ABOUT THE AUTHOR

Meet Mishica Moon, the beloved primary school teacher and children's author from London. As a child, she loved books and storytelling, which led her to pursue a career in education. Mishica's unique teaching methods and love for her students inspired her to write children's books that reflect their diverse experiences and contain important messages. She believes all stories have something to teach us. When she's not writing or teaching, Mishica advocates for education and literacy. Her books transport readers to magical lands and remind them of the magic in the world. Anything is possible with the imagination!

Thank you to all the amazing
children I've taught

Text and images by Mishica Moon

First published 2024

The rights of Mishica Moon are to
be identified as the author of this work.

All rights reserved. No part of this publication may be reproduced, stored in a retrieval system or reproduced or transmitted in any form or by any means, electronic, mechanical, photocopying, recording or otherwise, without prior consent.

Introduction

Welcome to…
"READING ROCKS:
25 Tips to Get Kids Hooked on Books!"

Reading is like magic on paper!
It can take you to unknown destinations, meet amazing people, and teach you things you didn't know. But sometimes, getting into books can be tricky for some children.
That's where Reading Rocks comes in!
This book is about helping children discover and maintain the joy of reading, as getting them excited about picking up a book can be challenging in today's tablet-driven world.
You'll find a bounty of easy and practical tips in this book. These tips focus on making reading a fun experience so that your child will develop a lifelong love for books.
Let's start the adventure of making books a beloved part of every child's life!

Let's go!

Knowing where to start or how to encourage children to enjoy books can take time and effort.
Some children might love stories about superheroes, while others might get lost in tales about football, animals, dinosaurs, or faraway lands.
What matters most is finding what makes their little hearts race and their eyes light up.
The tips within the following pages are for anyone who wants to help children find the joy of reading.
Reading Rocks can be 'cherry-picked' with children or used as a resource to help them.
You will discover ideas for making reading fun and exciting in cosy reading spots, using silly voices, and even getting your child to create their own stories!
Are you ready for discovery?

Tip 1
Start Early

Guess what?
You can start this magical journey right from day one!
Even when your little munchkin is just a tiny bundle, you can plant a seed of curiosity that organically grows into a love for books. Reading to your baby, showing them colourful pictures, and letting them hear your voice can make a big difference in future habits.
While they can't read, they can learn and recognise auditory patterns.

Tip 2
Be a Reading Role Model

Children will get curious when they see adults around them with a book, especially in the home environment.
They will reach for books for themselves in no time. It is important that grown-ups read books in front of their children.
You can be a reading role model, and you can share and read your favourite childhood books with them.
Maybe discuss the stories and share fun parts.
In doing this, you show that reading is fun.
Also, you could create family reading time, where everyone reads their favourite book in the same room.

Tip 3
Create a Reading-Friendly Environment

Have you ever been to a Reading Wonderland?
First, find a spot in your home, whether a cosy nook, a corner of your bedroom, or a space in the living room where your child can snuggle up with a good book. Maybe you could drape a mesh over the area to give it that wonderland appeal. This could be their special reading place, where they can disappear into the pages of a favourite book.
Next, add soft pillows or a beanbag chair for them to sink into, and don't forget a furry blanket to wrap themselves in while they read.
Now, you can fill their corner with their favourite stories, picture books, and anything else that interests them.
After that, add fun decorations to make the reading corner come alive. Draw pictures or get your child to draw pictures. You can even hang up photos of their favourite book characters, string fairy lights around the space for a cosy glow, or scatter some stuffed animals to accompany your child while they read.

Tip 4
Read Aloud Together

Using intonation when you read is priceless.

Reading aloud is like painting pictures with words and sounds! This is the best way to make stories come alive. Teach your child what makes a good reader and encourage them to change their voice when reading a particular character. Where necessary, pause to talk about specific words, use punctuation, and ask questions about what may come next. Share and exchange your thoughts and feelings. Reading aloud isn't just for bedtime; you can do it anytime!

Caregivers, take turns reading with your child and celebrate their intonation efforts. For older kids, you can act out scenes or help them create their own stories.

Reading aloud together creates sweet memories, and I'm sure there will be many giggles along the way. So, pick a book, gather your loved ones, and dive into those characters!

Tip 5
Let Children Choose Their Own Books

Put your little bookworms in charge of their reading adventures. Let them pick the stories they want to explore, like tales about football, dinosaurs, princesses, space adventures, or magical kingdoms. Caregivers, allow your child to experience a variety of books by taking them to the library or bookstore.

Also, keep various books at home so your child can choose based on their mood and interests. You empower children when you let them choose their books. It's part of their maturity; they feel independent and excited to start a new adventure. Talk about the books and their choices, and share their excitement.

Remember, there's no right or wrong choice—let them take full control of their reading journey. Additionally, letting children choose their own books not only helps them develop a love for reading but also shows them that their voices matter.

Tip 6

Make Reading Fun

Reading is an absolute blast!
You can make it as fun as a day out at a funfair! Here's how: Play quiz games through reading and comprehension; if your child answers correctly, they get a reward. Also, turn reading into a family game with "story charades" to make it interactive and exciting.
Use props and costumes to immerse your child in the story, and mix up reading materials with comics, magazines, or even signs while on a walk.
Why not create theme days where you explore books about a certain topic and celebrate reading milestones with parties or rewards?
Caregivers, reading should be as exciting as playing sports or going on an adventure, so grab a book and turn reading time into a crazy ride of fun and imagination!

Tip 7
Use Technology Wisely

Who says gadgets are just for games?
There are some super cool apps and websites that bring stories to life! Technology can make reading even more fun by offering an exciting interactive library at your fingertips! Reading apps allow you to explore endless worlds and adventures at home, in the car, or on holidays.

Some websites enable you to borrow eBooks and listen to audiobooks, in which the stories are read aloud by actors or authors. Caregivers, be mindful of using technology wisely. You may even take the opportunity to teach your child about "stranger danger" online. Limit your child's screen time and choose safe, age-appropriate content.

Caregivers and their little ones can explore apps and websites together. Technology can ignite your child's imagination and turn your device into another dimension with limitless adventures.

Tip 8

Explore Different Genres

Dive headfirst into stories and discover new worlds!

Imagine a giant treasure chest filled with every kind of book you can imagine, each like a different package waiting to be unveiled. From funny capers to spooky mysteries, there's something for everyone.

Explore different genres, such as comedy, fantasy, mystery, adventure, science fiction, historical fiction, and realistic fiction. Each genre is unique and offers a chance for a new experience.

Tip 9

Visit the Library Regularly

Why don't you get a library card and head for a treasure hunt of wall-to-wall books with mysterious adventures? Discover picture books, chapter books, comics, anime, and non-fiction delights. You can even book storytime sessions, craft workshops, and movie nights for fun events for children.

Explore the shelves with your child and help them make new friends. Caregivers, make library visits a weekly trip, and get your child to ask librarians for recommendations. It is important to remember that borrowing books empowers and teaches responsibility and respect for property.

Tip 10
Join a Book Club or Reading Group

Joining a book club is like throwing a book party where people enjoy their favourite stories!

Find one that matches your child's interests at school, library, or bookstore. Through discussing books at home with your child, and in the book club, they can discuss a different book at each meeting, share thoughts, and make new friends.

Book clubs also offer activities like movie nights and author visits. Caregivers, encourage your child to join for socialising, communication skills, and new reading experiences.

Tip ||

Incorporate Books into Daily Activities

You can take books everywhere you go, adding bookish fun to daily adventures!

Incorporate them into shopping, cooking, holidays, car trips, or outdoor activities. Choose book themes according to what you're doing, like a cookbook with fun recipes or a story about animals for a walk in the park.

Use books to inspire creative activities, like making treasure maps and building rocket ships or replicas of planets.

Grown-ups, slip reading into your child's evening routine so it's a natural part of your child's day.

Adding books to daily activities turns ordinary moments into special ones and sparks imagination and curiosity!

Tip 12

Encourage Writing and Storytelling

Is your child a budding storyteller? They have the power to create magical worlds. Give your child a pencil and watch their imagination soar! Children have a great imagination, and writing and storytelling skills are superpowers! Let them start by discussing the story they want to tell. Encourage them to think about a beginning, middle, and strong ending, and watch their magic happen! Then, don't worry too much about spelling, handwriting, etc. Just get your child to start free writing! Share their stories with friends and family to show pride and inspire others.

Tip 13

Celebrate Reading Milestones

All reading achievements are worth celebrating! Whether your child has read one word, three words, a page or two, finished a book, or improved by a level, take a moment to get them to pat themselves on the back. Track your child's progress with a milestone chart and reward them.

To celebrate the achievement, you could create a reading party playlist to dance and sing along to. You could also capture the moment with photos for a scrapbook or album.

Celebrating reading milestones is about recognising hard work and love for books. So, throw a party with confetti and cupcakes for your child's achievement!

Tip 14
Connect Reading to Real-Life Experiences

Reading is about more than escaping; sometimes, it's about understanding our connections to the world. You could start with books that mirror your culture or experiences and then branch out to explore other cultures. Ask your child to discuss how the stories relate to their life.

Connecting reading to real life helps your child see the world more clearly. It opens their eyes to new possibilities.

Tip 15

Read the Same Book Together

Sharing a book with a friend is like sharing an adventure in a secret club!
Get your child to invite a friend for a sleepover, have them choose a book they both love, and let them read it together.
Listen as they share thoughts and feelings.
This is good for bonding over a love of reading and learning from peers, as it strengthens reading skills.

Tip 16

Encourage Reading Beyond Books

Reading isn't limited to books—a whole world of reading is waiting to be unveiled and explored!
You can also dive into comics, magazines, and newspapers for exciting adventures!

Tip 17

Support Reluctant Readers

So, what types of books is my child into?
You can start by exploring different genres to see what resonates with your child. Whether they're into action-packed animal tales or heartwarming stories of friendship, there's a book waiting for them. If traditional books aren't their thing, consider graphic novels, comics, or magazines—they blend words and pictures for a more dynamic, accessible read.
Encourage your child to ask for help if they feel stuck and remind them that support is available every step of the way.
Supporting reluctant readers is like embarking on an epic quest, with exciting discoveries awaiting.

Tip 18

Make Reading a Social Activity

How can you make reading even more fun for your child?

Turn it into a reading party with their friends! These parties bring the coolest stories to life with their favourite people. Gather your child's friends for a reading party—set up a cosy nook, bring their favourite books, and take turns reading aloud or quietly enjoying stories.

You could also organise a book swap where each friend brings a wrapped book to trade. It'll be like a treasure hunt for new stories.

Afterwards, they can enjoy party snacks while discussing their favourite parts of the books, characters, and plot twists. It's a chance to bond with friends and discover new stories together!

Tip 19

Foster a Love for Libraries and Bookstores

Libraries and bookstores are colourful, magical places full of treasures. You could make visiting them a regular family outing. These places are where the love for reading can take root and blossom. With endless rows of books and the chance to create cherished family memories, you can make exploring libraries and bookstores a tradition.

Tip 20

Encourage Reading Diverse Voices

Discover the wonder of diverse stories! Books from various authors and cultures offer a rich depth of experience. They take us to uncharted territories, broaden our horizons, and celebrate the diversity of our beautiful world. You can encourage your child to embrace these voices and foster empathy and understanding through stories.

Tip 21
Make Reading a Family Tradition

Start a super cool tradition: reading outside together as a family!
How about everyone grabbing a book for the annual holiday? It will add another magical dimension to quality family time. Not only does gathering with books at bedtime create lasting memories, but from breakfast time to beach trips, weaving reading into family rituals brings family members closer together.

Tip 22

Keep Reading Positive

Sometimes, reading can feel like solving a thousand-piece puzzle of a blue sky-frustrating and challenging.
But every page turned and understood is progress. Like cheering for a champion, encourage your reluctant child to keep pushing forward in their reading journey.
Remind them that each page brings them closer to the finish line!

Tip 23

Embrace Audio Books

Hey, have you ever tried audiobooks?
With an audiobook, your child can experience the magic of a story in a different way.
It's like handpicking a storyteller just for them!
Imagine someone with just the right voice to deliver a story— all they have to do is listen and tune into their imagination. Let the story unfold in their mind as they relax.
Your child can listen to an audiobook of their favourite story in the car, on the way to or from school, while relaxing, doing chores, or winding down before bed.

Tip 24

Create a Reading Fort

Why not turn reading time into an exciting adventure by building a reading fort?

Children will absolutely love it! Gather blankets, pillows, and cushions to construct a fort where your child can escape into the pages of their favourite books, undisturbed. You can drape the blankets over chairs and tables to create a cosy hideaway.

You could even add fairy lights to give the fort a mystical element and fill it with stuffed animals for comfort and company. Also, you could have your child design their own flag to make it feel more personal, like a special clubhouse. This little reading fort will make storytime feel extra special.

Tip 25

Storybook Scavenger Hunt

Here's another great idea! How about a storybook scavenger hunt? This is a fun way to make reading interactive and exciting. Start by choosing one of your child's favourite books. Next, hide items related to the book around the house or garden, then challenge your child to find each item and guess the book's name. This activity gives your child the chance to make connections and be resourceful!

To add even more fun, you can provide clues. This will encourage them to read, understand, and think deeply about the stories. Depending on your child's age and ability, you can simplify the scavenger hunt or make it more challenging.

Once they've found all the items, you can sit together and talk about the book and its connections to the items. It's a great way to spend quality time together while making reading an adventure!

Conclusion

As we bid farewell to our 25 tips, remember that no matter what book you're reading, there's always something interesting between the covers.

As your child continues their reading journey through the world of books, may their imagination expand, their curiosity grow, and their love for reading blossom like the tallest and brightest sunflower. Remember, the world is out there to discover, and with a stack of books in hand, there are no limits!

Happy reading! 📚✨

Thank you for reading "READING ROCKS: 25 Tips to Get Kids Hooked on Books!"
Readers mean a lot to me because your support encourages me to write more.
If you enjoyed "READING ROCKS: 25 Tips to Get Kids Hooked on Books!" please leave a review on Goodreads.
It will help other readers take a chance on this book or others.
Happy reading, and thank you again for being part of the Mishica Moon adventure!
Check out mishicamoonbooks – https://www.mishicamoonbooks.com